North American
INDIAN NATIONS

NATIVE PEOPLES
of the
GREAT BASIN

Krystyna Poray Goddu

LERNER PUBLICATIONS ◆ MINNEAPOLIS

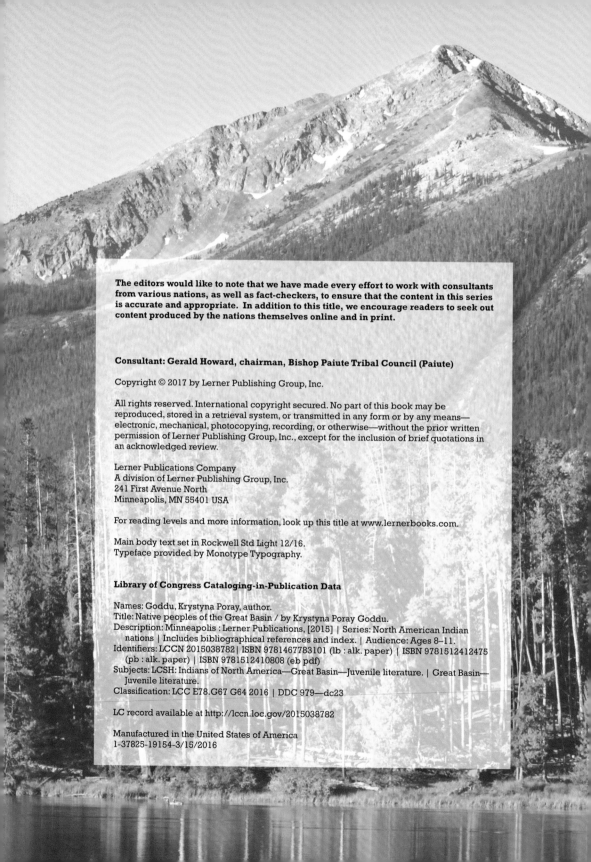

The editors would like to note that we have made every effort to work with consultants from various nations, as well as fact-checkers, to ensure that the content in this series is accurate and appropriate. In addition to this title, we encourage readers to seek out content produced by the nations themselves online and in print.

Consultant: Gerald Howard, chairman, Bishop Paiute Tribal Council (Paiute)

Lerner Publications Company
A division of Lerner Publishing Group, Inc.
241 First Avenue North
Minneapolis, MN 55401 USA

For reading levels and more information, look up this title at www.lernerbooks.com.

Main body text set in Rockwell Std Light 12/16.
Typeface provided by Monotype Typography.

Library of Congress Cataloging-in-Publication Data

Names: Goddu, Krystyna Poray, author.
Title: Native peoples of the Great Basin / by Krystyna Poray Goddu.
Description: Minneapolis : Lerner Publications, [2015] | Series: North American Indian
   nations | Includes bibliographical references and index. | Audience: Ages 8–11.
Identifiers: LCCN 2015038782| ISBN 9781467783101 (lb : alk. paper) | ISBN 9781512412475
   (pb : alk. paper) | ISBN 9781512410808 (eb pdf)
Subjects: LCSH: Indians of North America—Great Basin—Juvenile literature. | Great Basin—
   Juvenile literature.
Classification: LCC E78.G67 G64 2016 | DDC 979—dc23

LC record available at http://lccn.loc.gov/2015038782

Manufactured in the United States of America
1-37825-19154-3/15/2016

CONTENTS

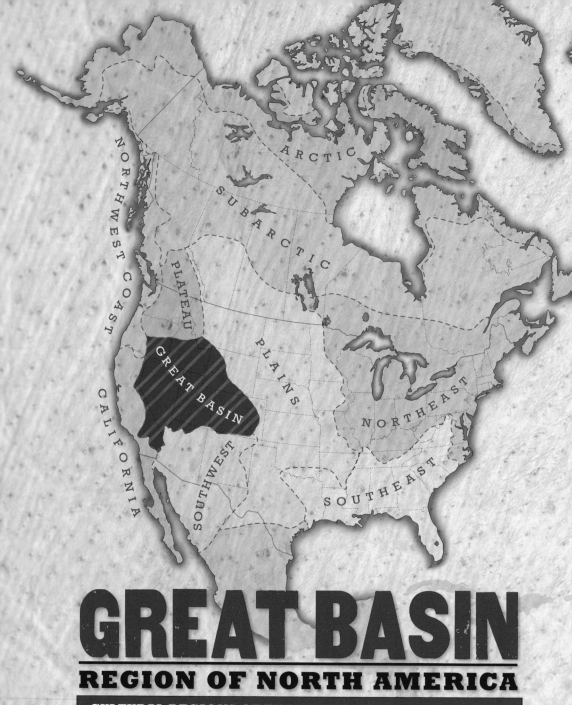

GREAT BASIN

REGION OF NORTH AMERICA

CULTURAL REGIONS OF THE UNITED STATES AND CANADA

- Plateau
- Northwest Coast
- California
- Plains
- Southeast
- Southwest
- Great Basin
- Northeast
- Subarctic
- Arctic
- Other

- - - Cultural area border
- International border
- State/province border

INTRODUCTION

Long ago, only Sinawav, the creator, and Coyote lived on Earth. When it was time to create more people, Sinawav gave Coyote a bag of sticks and told him to carry it to the sacred grounds. He would not tell Coyote what was in the bag.

But Coyote was curious. As he traveled, he decided to look into the bag. He opened the bag, and people came rushing out. They spoke languages Coyote did not understand. He tried to catch them. But they ran away. Coyote continued to the sacred grounds and let the few people left out of the bag. These people were the Ute (YOOT).

Coyote went back to Sinawav. The creator put a curse on him but said that the Ute would be brave and mighty.

This is the story the Ute tell about how they came to live in the Great Basin. The Great Basin is a giant bowl-shaped area made by valleys and mountains in the western United States. It includes most of Nevada and Utah and large parts of Oregon, Idaho, Wyoming, and Colorado. Small parts of Arizona, Montana, and California are in the Great Basin too. Rain and snow collect in this area, just like water fills a basin, or sink. This is because there are no rivers or streams leading out of the Great Basin into the

PEOPLES OF THE GREAT BASIN

The Great Basin region is the traditional homeland of many American Indian nations. This map shows the areas where some of them lived before Europeans arrived in the region.

CULTURAL AREAS

- Plateau
- Northwest Coast
- California
- Plains
- Southwest
- Great Basin

- - - Cultural area border
— International border
········· State/province border

Gulf of Mexico or the Pacific Ocean. Summers in the Great Basin are hot, and winters are freezing. The landscape is made up of mountains and deserts. The Great Basin is one of the hardest environments in North America to live in.

Many scientists who study the past say that the first people to live on this land spoke a Numic (NUHM-ik) language. These people were made up of many different groups. Some of the best-known nations in the Great Basin are the Shoshone (sho-SHO-nee) (which includes the Western, Eastern, Southern, and Northern Shoshone), the Ute, the Paiute (PIE-yoot), the Gosiute

WHAT THE GREAT BASIN NATIONS CALLED THEMSELVES

EUROPEAN NAME	NATION'S NAME	MEANING
Bannock	Bana'kwut	Water people
Paiute	Numa	People
Shoshone	Newe	People
Washoe	Wašiw	The people from here

(GOH-shoot), and the Bannock (BAH-nuk). These peoples didn't all speak the exact same language. But their languages were all based on the Uto-Aztecan (yoo-toh-AZ-teh-kuhn) language of Mexico. The Washoe (WASH-oh), another well-known Great Basin nation, spoke a Hokan (HO-kuhn) language.

The Great Basin area is surrounded by mountains. The Sierra Nevada is to the west. The Rocky Mountains are to the east. The peoples who lived in the Great Basin were isolated from other American Indian nations and even from other Great Basin nations. The different Shoshone nations lived in Nevada, Utah, Idaho, Wyoming, and Montana. The Bannock first lived in southeastern Oregon. Eventually they moved to the valleys of the Snake and Lemhi Rivers in Idaho. The Ute mostly lived in Utah, Colorado, and northern New Mexico. Parts of California, Nevada, Oregon, Arizona, and Utah were all home to the Paiute peoples. The areas south and west of Great Salt Lake in Utah were the land of the Gosiute. The Washoe land was in Nevada and California, around Lake Tahoe.

Many peoples of the Great Basin had to travel often to find food. As the seasons changed, groups of people moved from place to place. Most of their actions and decisions were focused on survival. They were always searching for food. They traveled and lived in small groups called bands. These bands were made up of thirty to one hundred people. These small groups made it easier to travel and to quickly build and take down their shelters.

Much of the Great Basin landscape is desert. The weather here is harsh, and resources were often scarce.

Most of the Great Basin nations traveled on foot. But in the seventeenth century, Spanish explorers in New Mexico introduced horses to the Southern Ute and the Eastern Shoshone. By 1700, these nations used horses to travel, hunt, trade, and go to war. They also brought horses to other nations. By 1800, the Northern Shoshone, Northern Paiute, and Northern and Central Ute nations used horses too. Other nations began using horses throughout the second half of the nineteenth century. The Washoe were the last ones to begin using horses.

Their isolation meant that the peoples of the Great Basin were among the last of the American Indians to meet Euro-Americans. This contact began in the early nineteenth century. The lives of Great Basin Indians would be changed forever. By the middle of the nineteenth century, many nations were being forced to give up their lands and move to reservations.

Despite this move, the Great Basin Indians never lost their connection to the land and their past. They continue to live throughout the area and pass their traditions from generation to generation.

CHAPTER 1

A HARSH
LANDSCAPE

The native peoples of the Great Basin learned how to survive its harsh climate and landscape. They passed their knowledge of the land from generation to generation. Each nation was familiar with its own lands and knew how to live on them. However, the overall population of the Great Basin Indians was rarely larger than forty thousand. This was because so little food was available and it took a lot of work to get it.

Food

The most common food throughout the Great Basin was the piñon, or the pine nut. Pine nuts grew in forests throughout the Great Basin. Every autumn the people traveled in bands to gather as many pine nuts as they could.

The pine nut forests throughout the Great Basin were an important source of food for the native peoples in the region.

These nuts were filled with protein. The people shelled, dried, and ate them. People of the Great Basin also picked seeds and berries. They dug roots and tubers out of the ground. They roasted grasshoppers and ground them into flour. Some Paiute groups were able to grow nut grass and wild hyacinth on lands watered by mountain snow. The native peoples also hunted small game such as rabbits, birds, rats, and lizards. Some hunted buffalo, sheep, elk, antelope, and deer.

GATHERING PINE NUTS

Pine nuts were a major food source for all the Great Basin peoples. Gathering the pine nuts was an important event each year. Throughout the rest of the year, families followed the animals they hunted or went to areas where plants were growing. The pine nut harvest was one of the only times when large groups would gather. Pine nuts were ripe in September, so every autumn, bands settled together for several months. They built huts near the pine nut forests. Men, women, and children worked together to gather and save food for the winter. The nuts could be eaten raw, pounded into flour, or turned into a mush. Nations such as the Northern Paiute still hold an annual festival to celebrate the pine nut harvest. The festival includes a traditional pine nut blessing dance.

The Shoshone were sometimes known as Elk Eaters after they began hunting large game.

After the Ute got horses, hunting became much easier. Large game became a big part of the Ute diet. The Shoshone also ate sheep, elk, and buffalo. They became known as Sheep Eaters, Elk Eaters, or Buffalo Eaters. Other nations were known by the food they ate too. The Paiute were called Wild Onion Eaters, Yellow-Bellied Marmot Eaters, and Ground Squirrel Eaters. The Bannock were known as Buffalo Eaters and Honey Eaters.

Homes

Great Basin families lived in shelters that were easy to put up and take down. In warm weather, they built round brush shelters from whatever materials they could find. These materials might include sagebrush, willow, leaves, or grass. The brush shelters were not meant to last.

When the weather grew colder, Great Basin peoples built sturdier homes called wickiups. They first built a domed frame from willow tree branches. They covered the frame with reeds, branches, and grass. Sometimes they added bark and soil for more protection. Often they also piled rocks around the base of the hut. This helped keep warmth inside. At the very top of the wickiup, there was a hole so that smoke from the fire inside could escape.

Some of the Shoshone nations camped in areas that had lots of grass for their horses. This tall grass was called *sosoni*. This grass is probably how the Shoshone got their name. The Shoshone built cone-shaped homes from sosoni. Other nations began to call them the Grass House People.

Many Great Basin Indians made domed shelters from branches and grass.

Clothing

Summers were so hot that men often did not wear clothes. Women wore aprons made from buckskin or from strips of sagebrush, juniper bark, or yucca. The aprons were held on by braided cords or belts. Men and women often went barefoot. But sometimes they wore woven sandals.

During the very cold months, both men and women wore robes made from bison fur or rabbit skins. They might also weave robes from plants such as sagebrush bark and tule (a tall, spiky plant that grows in wetlands). They wore fur caps too. Snowshoes had a round or oval frame made from small branches. They covered the frame with woven buckskin.

Under their robes, men wore breechcloths. These had a flap in front and a flap in back. They were held in place by a belt at the waist. Breechcloths were made from grass, shredded bark, or

Great Basin peoples wore clothing made from animal skin, bark, and grass. Men often wore a breechcloth, like the one shown here.

deerskin. If the people had deerskin, they also made leggings from it. Sometimes men wore hip-length tunics instead of breechcloths. The tunics were made from rabbit skin, woven grass, or shredded bark. Women added a second apron with a tunic or poncho on top. If they had buckskin, they made dresses with fringed sleeves and hems.

Clothing for the Great Basin peoples was meant to be practical. Besides fringes, the only other decorations might be feathers or jewelry made from beads or shells. But after the Euro-Americans arrived, the Great Basin Indians began to use more decorations, especially beadwork, on their clothes.

CHAPTER 2

SOCIETY AND
SPIRITUALITY

Most of the Great Basin Indians lived in family **groups.** Typically, these groups were made up of the mother, father, and children. Sometimes grandparents, uncles, or aunts lived with the family too. Among the Paiute and Northern Shoshone peoples, if there were few women, sometimes two brothers shared a wife.

Families lived and traveled together in bands. They shared the tasks necessary for survival. Children were taught at an early age to help with food gathering, but the mother and father usually gathered most of the food. Grandparents often took care of the young children.

In some nations, families arranged marriages. But the

Children in Great Basin nations learned from a young age to help gather food.

Family was very important to the Great Basin Indians. Each member of the family worked together to gather food and perform other tasks necessary for survival.

Paiute had a special tradition for a man to follow when he wanted to marry a woman. Young unmarried women often slept next to their grandmothers. If a young man wanted to marry a woman, he would come into the family home at night and sleep at the woman's feet. If she did not want to marry him, she left her grandmother's side and slept by her mother instead.

In general, marriage ceremonies were informal. In some nations, the two families gave each other gifts. In other nations, if a man and a woman started to live together, this meant they were married. Often the couple would live with the bride's parents for the first few years of marriage. But they were free to leave and join another band, especially when there was not a lot of food. Divorce was common among Great Basin peoples. Like the marriage ceremony, divorce was informal.

Leadership

Most Great Basin nations did not have a formal government, structure, or leaders. People could join or leave bands easily. Usually people would follow a leader for as long as he could find food. Some nations had informal leaders. Among the Paiute, the *niave,* or leader, led by example. He was not the decision maker. But during meetings, he might give suggestions and advice to help the nation make a decision as a group. The Northern Shoshone had a *daigwahni.* This means "talker." The daigwahni's main job was to know when different wild plants were getting ripe and to tell his people. The daigwahni was usually a strong and convincing speaker.

Many Great Basin nations had a leader to help make decisions about where to go to find food. This Southern Ute leader may have had a more formal leadership role.

Because the Ute began using horses early, they were able to travel farther and meet more people. When they came in contact with native peoples of the Plains, they began to take on many Plains Indian practices. The Ute culture became more warlike, and leadership roles became more formal. The Ute had a chief spokesman and a civil chief who ruled over their daily lives. When they went to war, they might also have a war chief.

Spirituality

Like most American Indians, the Great Basin Indians believed that everything in nature has a spirit. They believed that people, animals, trees, and plants have spirits. Mountains, rivers, and even the sun and rain had a spirit too. A spiritual leader communicated with the spirit world.

Most American Indians have a story that explains how the world was made. This story often describes how a creator

The Great Basin could often be a harsh area, but Great Basin Indians still had great respect for the nature around them as they believed everything had a spirit.

took on the shape of an animal or a part of nature to create the world. Many Great Basin Indians tell stories about two powerful beings, Wolf and his brother, Coyote. Wolf is the most powerful and is wise and respected. He is often called the father and creator of the world. Coyote is a trickster. But Coyote also created many parts of nature and Great Basin culture. In some Great Basin stories, it is said that Wolf created the solar system and all people. In others, Coyote spread peoples throughout the Great Basin region. Some nations say that the world was covered in water, and Wolf and Coyote created the world from mud. But in general, Great Basin peoples have fewer stories about creation than about death and how the world will end. In one of these stories, it is said that Wolf did not want people to die. But Coyote said that they must die. When Coyote's son dies, he tries to change his

Wolves are present in many of the stories of Great Basin Indians. Often the wolf represents a wise and respected being.

RITUALS OF THE GREAT BASIN INDIANS

PEOPLE	CEREMONY	PURPOSE
Ute	Bear dance	To provide strength for hunting bears
Southern Paiute	Mourning or cry ceremony	To end formal mourning periods for the dead
Shoshone	Sun Dance	To bring healing and harmony to the community
Northern Paiute	Ghost Dance	To bring back ancestors and the traditional way of life
All Great Basin peoples	Round dance	To give thanks for food

mind. Wolf does not let Coyote stop death. In the Shoshone story, death is a punishment for Coyote's tricks.

The most important ceremony for the Great Basin peoples was the round dance. This was the only ceremony some nations took part in each year. In the round dance, people held hands and danced around a tree or pole. While they danced, they gave thanks for whatever food they ate most. In autumn, they might give thanks for the pine nut harvest or the first rabbit hunt. In the spring, they might give thanks for the first antelope hunt.

Each group of Great Basin Indians practiced its own ritual when a person died. The Shoshone buried their dead in rock-covered graves. The Ute were also buried and their belongings were destroyed or given away. The Washoe burned the dead and their homes. When they were mourning, the Paiute cut their hair. A widow would cut her hair first. Then other relatives of the person who died cut off their hair too. A Paiute widow was not allowed to marry again until her hair had grown back.

Medicine

When Great Basin Indians were sick, they called on medicine people, or healers. Men or women could be healers. They used a variety of methods for healing. Herbs and plants, including roots and bark, were used as medicine. Stomach problems, for example, were treated with teas made from herbs. A medicine man or woman might also call out to the spirit of an animal or sing songs. Sacred carvings called fetishes were also used in

A Ute rock carving of a spiritual leader, or medicine person

healing as they were believed to grant power and protection.

Often healers performed rituals or chanted to cure the sick person. Marie Lehi, a Southern Paiute woman, remembered watching her grandfather, a Paiute medicine man, perform healing rituals. "He used to use the eagle for medicine," she said. "He would suck out the evil from the body. The evil was a kind of spirit. . . . I used to watch him when he would sing medicine songs over the patient. Another spirit of his was the flying squirrel. He never killed an eagle or flying squirrel but just prayed to them singing, and the people got well."

CHAPTER 3

MAKING ART

Like other American Indians, the Great Basin peoples made everything they needed. They made clothing, tools, and weapons. They also made art. But the Great Basin nations moved often. So their art had to be useful and easy to move. Great Basin peoples are best known for their woven baskets. These baskets were a necessary part of their daily lives.

Great Basin Indians made art that was also useful, like this Ute gathering basket.

Basketmaking

Baskets were used for gathering and storing food and carrying babies and supplies. These types of baskets were called burden baskets. They were woven from plants such as willow, sagebrush, reeds, and ferns. The Great Basin peoples were skilled at weaving these materials so tightly that the baskets could hold tiny seeds and even water. Basketmaking skills were practiced mostly by women and were passed down through the generations. Young girls learned by watching their mothers and grandmothers weave. Each nation had its own unique style of basket.

MODERN GREAT BASIN BASKET WEAVERS

ARTIST	PEOPLE	STYLE
Florine Conway	Washoe	Coiled round baskets
Lilly Sanchez	Western Shoshone	Twined burden baskets
Everett Pikyavit	Southern Paiute	Coiled bowls
Evelyn Pete	Shoshone	Twined waterproof water baskets
Larena Burns	Paiute-Washoe	Round pine needle baskets

Washoe basket weaver Dat-So-La-Lee weaving her unique round baskets

One of the most famous basket weavers was from the Washoe Nation. Washoe baskets were especially prized by buyers. One Washoe woman, Dat-So-La-Lee (ca. 1829–1925), created a round basket style called *degikup*. The degikup were often used to hold pine nut soup and other foods. The baskets were also important for Washoe ceremonies. During a dance, the baskets might be given to the singers and dancers as a gift of thanks. Dat-So-La-Lee began making baskets when the craft was starting to die out. Her work helped bring back interest in weaving. She continues to be an inspiration for modern craftspeople.

Jewelry and Beadwork

The Great Basin peoples made earrings and necklaces of shells, seeds, feathers, and bones. After meeting Plains Indians in the nineteenth century, some nations such as the Ute and the Shoshone began adding beads to their jewelry. The Shoshone especially are known for their beadwork. They decorated dresses, belts, and moccasins with beads made from seeds, animal teeth, or bones. After they met and began trading with Euro-Americans in the nineteenth century, the Great Basin Indians began using glass beads too. They created geometric and floral patterns to decorate clothing, footwear, bags, and cradleboards.

Animals and Crafts

The Shoshone painted pictures of important events such as dances or hunts on animal skins. They often used the skins

This Ute deer hide dress is decorated with geometric beadwork.

of buffalo or elk. The Shoshone used natural materials such as charcoal and red ochre to make color. But through trade, the Shoshone later began using paint and dye from the Euro-Americans instead. Some Shoshone and Paiute also carved pictures into rock. These pictures are called petroglyphs. Sometimes these images might show dances, hunts, or battles.

But many times they were carved for spiritual reasons. The carvings could show mythical beings or important animals. They may have been a way to help Great Basin Indians connect with the spirits and to ask for rain or a successful hunt. The Great Basin is home to the largest petroglyph sites in North America.

The Shoshone peoples who lived in the mountains were also known for making powerful bows from animal horns. They made these bows by heating and straightening the horns. They then joined the horns together and wrapped them with rawhide. The process took about two months. The bows were between 18 and 24 inches (46 to 61 centimeters) long. They were powerful

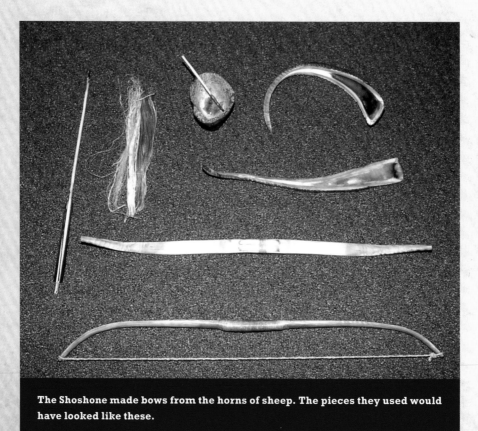

The Shoshone made bows from the horns of sheep. The pieces they used would have looked like these.

The Northern Paiute used duck decoys such as these to help them hunt birds.

enough to send an arrow through a bison. When the Shoshone traded with other nations, these bows were greatly prized. One bow could be traded for a horse and a gun.

The Northern Paiute created real-looking duck decoys to help them hunt birds. They bundled and tied tule reed to look just like a duck. These decoys floated on marshes and tricked ducks and other birds into landing by them. Hunters then shot the birds with their bow and arrows.

CHAPTER 4

DISRUPTED LIVES

The Great Basin Indians met Europeans later than many other American Indians. The Southern Ute met Spanish explorers in the early seventeenth century. But most of the Great Basin nations did not see Europeans until the nineteenth century.

People Push West

In 1803, President Thomas Jefferson bought land from France that stretched from the Mississippi River to the Rocky Mountains. This was known as the Louisiana Purchase. European explorers and traders moved to the area. Other American Indians moved there too. They wanted to find new land for trapping beavers and other animals. They would then be able to sell the fur to the Europeans. These fur traders quickly wiped out the supply of beavers in the Great Basin. The fur traders left the area and headed farther west.

In 1847, a large group of Mormons, or members of the Church of Jesus Christ of Latter-day Saints, arrived in Ute and Paiute territories. The Mormons were looking for an isolated

One of the most famous Great Basin Indians was a Shoshone named Sacagawea. She was born in the late 1780s. When she was about eleven years old, she was kidnapped and raised by a band of Hidatsa, a Plains Indian nation. Eventually a fur trader named Toussaint Charbonneau bought her. She gave birth to his child in 1804. The explorers Meriwether Lewis and William Clark hired Charbonneau as a guide and translator. Charbonneau brought along Sacagawea and their son. Sacagawea was familiar with the land, its plants, and American Indian languages. So she was able to help the explorers. When they needed horses, Sacagawea led them to a Shoshone village where her brother was a chief. Sacagawea was able to translate so the explorers could purchase horses from the Shoshone. Her and her child's presence with the explorers showed the American Indians they met that Lewis and Clark were on a peaceful mission. In 2000, the US Mint decided to show Sacagawea's image on the new gold dollar coin. This recognized the important role Sacagawea played in American history.

region where they could live peacefully. The Great Basin seemed perfect. The leader of the Mormons, Brigham Young, founded Salt Lake City in what is now Utah. Then he sent other Mormons to set up communities in the region.

Soon after the first Mormons arrived, gold was discovered

in California. Streams of people traveled through the Great Basin. They were hoping to get rich in California. Gold and silver were discovered in the Nevada Territory in 1859. Miners came to the region to stay. They were followed by engineers, bankers, and businesspeople. In 1864, Nevada became a US state.

A mining town in Nevada

Struggling to Survive

The lives of the Great Basin Indians changed dramatically as Euro-Americans began to settle in the region. Great Basin Indian land was turned into mines, ranches, and farms. Pine nut forests were cut down for building and firewood. Many nations fought back against the intruders. They tried to drive Euro-Americans away by attacking wagon trains and ranches. There were many conflicts between Euro-Americans and Great Basin Indians from the late 1840s through the 1870s. Many people on both sides died. The Euro-Americans also brought a sickness called cholera to the Great Basin. The Great Basin peoples had never been exposed to this disease before, so their bodies had not built up any immunity to it. Between 1850 and 1860, a cholera epidemic broke out, and even more Great Basin peoples died. By the time Euro-Americans came to the Great Basin region, the US

CONFLICTS BETWEEN THE US GOVERNMENT AND GREAT BASIN PEOPLES

PEOPLE	WAR OR BATTLE	CAUSE
Paiute	Pyramid Lake War of 1860	Many trading posts and pony express stations being set up in the region
Bannock	Bannock War of 1878	The destruction of land by Euro-Americans
Ute	Meeker Massacre of 1879	Ute land turned into farmland by government agent Nathan Meeker

government had forced American Indian peoples in other parts of the country to give up their land. The government let these peoples keep only small areas of land called reservations. Sometimes nations were forced to give up all their land. They had to move to reservations in other parts of the country.

The Great Basin peoples continued to be moved from their land in the second half of the nineteenth century. In 1859, the Pyramid Lake Paiute Tribe reservation was set up in Nevada. In 1868, the Shoshone and Bannock nations agreed to a treaty that gave them reservations in Wyoming and Idaho. In 1879, the US government and American Indians fought one of their most violent battles. It was called the Meeker Massacre. After this battle, the Ute were forced to give up their lands in Colorado and move to a reservation in Utah. By then, most of the Great Basin Indians were living on reservations.

Resisting Conversion

In 1890, a Northern Paiute medicine man known as Wovoka began performing what he called the Ghost Dance. He believed that the Ghost Dance would bring the dead back to life, drive away the Europeans, and let the Great Basin Indians live as they had in the past. The Ghost Dance became an important ritual for the Great Basin Indians. It spread to other American Indian nations in the West too. It continued to be performed into the twentieth century.

Euro-Americans often forced American Indians to give

The Ghost Dance became an important ritual for many American Indian nations, including the Arapaho in Oklahoma, shown here.

SARAH WINNEMUCCA (1844–1891)

Sarah Winnemucca was a Paiute woman who helped fight for the rights of her nation. She went to school in California. Then she returned to Nevada to be a teacher and translator between the Paiute and members of the US government. She began to speak out publicly against the way the Paiute were treated. Soon she became known as a strong activist for the Paiute people. She traveled the country giving speeches and wrote an autobiography called *Life among the Piutes: Their Wrongs and Claims*. She was one of the most famous American Indian women of her time.

up their religious traditions and convert to Christianity. Many Great Basin Indians resisted and never became Christians. But in the early twentieth century, one form of Christianity did take hold among some people of the Great Basin nations: the Native American Church. This church mixes American Indian and Christian ideas. The Native American Church is still active. Some of its ceremonies last all night and include praying and singing. In the morning, the people end the ceremony by having breakfast together.

CHAPTER 5

A CHANGED WORLD

By the end of the nineteenth century, most Great Basin Indians lived on reservations. Over time, the US government took portions of land away from the reservations and gave them to white Americans. The Great Basin Indians could no longer gather food as they always had. They had to work on farms or ranches owned by the American newcomers. The Great Basin peoples were no longer free to make their own decisions. They were under the control of the US government. Many American Indian children were sent away to boarding schools. At these schools, they had to learn English and were not allowed to speak their native languages.

Fighting for Rights and Land

In 1934, the US government passed the Indian Reorganization Act (IRA). The IRA allowed nations to create their own governments called tribal councils. These councils were set up similarly to the US form of government. Members of the councils were elected by the people of the nation. In the Great Basin region, these councils started ranching and tourism businesses. They also fought to get back the land that had been taken from them. In 1950, the US government recognized that the Ute had been illegally removed from their land in the nineteenth century. The Ute didn't get the land back. But they did receive money. In 1993, the Western Shoshone went to the United Nations to

GREAT BASIN POPULATIONS AS OF THE 2010 CENSUS

PEOPLE	ESTIMATED POPULATION
Fort Hall Tribal Grouping (Shoshone-Bannock)	5,428
Paiute tribal grouping	13,767
Paiute-Shoshone tribal grouping	4,379
Shoshone tribal grouping	13,002
Te-Moak Tribes of Western Shoshone Indians of Nevada tribal grouping	1,499
Ute tribal grouping	11,491
Washoe tribal grouping	2,058

*Census numbers according to those who identify as being part of these nations alone or in combination with one or more other nations.

fight for the return of some of the land that was taken from them. The United Nations declared in 2003 that the US government had ignored Shoshone rights and had not properly handled the conflict with the Western Shoshone.

Celebrating the Past

As of 2010, 78 percent of American Indians no longer lived on reservations. Many American Indian traditions are becoming less common. And some American Indian languages are in danger of disappearing. However, many Great Basin Indians do live on reservations. They work hard to preserve their traditions and to keep their native languages alive. Some nations have combined and share reservations. More than half of the Shoshone and Bannock peoples live on the Fort Hall Reservation

A sign in Utah welcomes visitors to the homelands of the Ute Indians.

in Idaho. The Duck Valley Indian Reservation is on the Idaho and Nevada border. It is shared by many Shoshone and Paiute.

Many Gosiute live on one of two reservations. These reservations are on the Utah–Nevada border or in Skull Valley, Utah. Many Ute live near Montrose, Colorado. About thirty-five hundred Ute live on reservations in Utah.

Great Basin nations are working to preserve their cultures in many ways. Some, such as the Shoshone-Bannock, regularly hold powwows. At powwows, people gather for drumming contests

A traditional dancer at a Shoshone-Bannock powwow

and dancing. The Paiute participate in festivals that include powwows, arts and crafts shows, and traditional foods.

Those living on the Fort Hall Reservation in Idaho are also working to preserve the Shoshone language. In 2013, a school in Fort Hall began teaching its kindergarten students using only the Shoshone language. Older students also received daily Shoshone lessons. The school hopes that children will become fluent in Shoshone and that this will help keep the language alive.

The Washoe also have many programs to preserve their culture. Historically, the Washoe gathered in late spring and summer around what is now known as Lake Tahoe. They believed the lake was sacred. The Washoe Cultural Resource Advisory Council encourages fishing, plant gathering, and basket weaving in the region around the lake. They also work to keep the Washoe language in use. The Washoe Tribe of Nevada and California runs the Meeks Bay Resort and Marina on Lake Tahoe. They hold an arts and crafts festival every summer. The Great Basin Native Basketweavers Association and the Nevada Arts Council's Folklife Apprenticeship Program

Historically, the Washoe believed Lake Tahoe to be sacred. The lake is still an important site for fishing and cultural activities.

CLYDE HALL

Clyde Hall is the director of the Naraya Cultural Preservation Council (NCPC). Hall is Shoshone-Métis (may-TEE). He has dedicated his life to the preservation of traditional ceremonies and knowledge. He was born and raised by his grandmother in a one-room log house on the Fort Hall Reservation. He has served the reservation's people as a lawyer in the tribal court and also worked as a high school teacher. He considers his greatest life work to be the renewal of the Great Basin and Plateau people's traditional Dance for All People. He is also one of the leaders of this ceremony. The Dance for All People brings together people of all races and religions to celebrate the protection and healing of the earth.

also work to keep Great Basin traditions, especially basket weaving, alive. These organizations offer classes in basket weaving. They also provide information and other opportunities to help current and future generations understand and pass on their heritage and culture.

Like many other American Indian nations, those of the Great Basin seek balance between living as American citizens and celebrating their past and traditions. In many ways, Great Basin Indians live similarly to other Americans. Yet they are proud of their heritage. They teach their languages, traditional crafts, and important rituals to the next generation, and they work for a better future.

Sue Coleman (Washoe)

is a basketmaker. In 2003, she received the Nevada Governor's Arts Award for Excellence in Folk and Traditional Arts. Coleman's work has been shown in museums and festivals across the country. She also teaches the craft to others, including her own daughter and granddaughter, to keep this important Washoe tradition alive.

Carrie and Mary Dann (Western Shoshone)

began fighting the US government for the return of Western Shoshone land in 1972. They said that the treaty signed in 1868 gave the United States the right to pass through the Shoshone land in Nevada but not to own it. For their work to preserve the traditional land, the Dann sisters received the international Right Livelihood Award in 1993. A film called *American Outrage* was made in 2008 about the Dann sisters' work.

Adrian C. Louis (Paiute)

has published numerous books of poetry and fiction that focus on American Indian life. His novel, *Skins*, was made into a film in 2002. Louis has also worked as a journalist and as a college professor in South Dakota and Minnesota. He was inducted into the Nevada Writers Hall of Fame in 1999.

Mark Trahant (Shoshone-Bannock)

is a well-known journalist who focuses on American Indian issues. In 1989, Trahant was a finalist for a Pulitzer Prize for national reporting for his series on federal Indian policy. He teaches at the University of Alaska Anchorage and the University of North Dakota. He also works to help the University of North Dakota strengthen relationships with tribal community colleges.

Timeline

Each Great Basin Indian culture had its own way of recording history. This timeline is based on the Gregorian calendar, which Europeans brought to North America.

Ca. 15 CE Numic-speaking peoples arrive in the region.

1600s: The Ute encounter Spanish explorers who introduce them to horses.

1800s The Shoshone and Bannock nations begin using horses.

1803 President Jefferson bought the Louisiana Territory, and Euro-Americans began to move west.

1810 Fur traders begin arriving in the Great Basin region.

1840s Europeans move into the Great Basin region.

1847 Mormons come to the Great Basin region.

1850–1860 The cholera epidemic kills many members of the Great Basin nations.

1859 Gold and silver are discovered in the Nevada Territory.

1860 The Shoshone, Bannock, and Paiute join forces against Euro-Americans in the Pyramid Lake War.

1879 The Meeker Massacre forces the Ute to leave Colorado and settle in Utah.

1890 The Ghost Dance movement is started by Northern Paiute Wovoka and spreads throughout American Indian tribes in the West.

1934 The Indian Reorganization Act establishes self-government for American Indian nations.

1950 Ute receive compensation from the US government for the land that was illegally taken from them.

2000 The US Mint recognizes Sacagawea's role in history by including her image on the new gold dollar coin.

2003 The UN declares that Washoe land had been illegally taken by the US government.

2015 The Paiute Indian Tribe of Utah celebrated the 35th Annual Paiute Restoration Gathering with a three-day powwow in Cedar City, Utah.

Glossary

activist: one who takes action in support of or against an issue

autobiography: a life story written by the person whom it is about

band: a small, family-based group within an American Indian nation

cholera: a serious disease that causes vomiting and diarrhea and often death

convert: to persuade someone to change from one belief to another

cradleboard: a padded wooden board used to carry babies

epidemic: a sudden, quickly spreading outbreak of a disease

Euro-American: someone living in the United States who is of European descent

isolated: separated from others

Louisiana Purchase: land bought from France by President Jefferson in 1803 that stretched from the Mississippi River to the Rocky Mountains

nation: an independent group of people with a shared history, culture, and governing system

petroglyph: a carving in a rock

powwow: a social gathering of American Indians that typically involves dancing

reservation: an area of land set aside by the US government for the use of an American Indian nation

translate: to change words from one language to another

treaty: an official agreement between two groups

Source Note

23 Susan H. Armitage, Patricia Hart, and Karen Weathermon, eds., *Women's Oral History: The Frontiers Reader* (Lincoln: University of Nebraska Press, 2002), 265.

Selected Bibliography

Canfield, Gae Whitney. *Sarah Winnemucca of the Northern Paiutes*. Norman: University of Oklahoma Press, 1988.

Debo, Angie. *A History of the Indians of the United States*. Norman: University of Oklahoma Press, 1970.

Moulton, Candy. *Everyday Life among the American Indians: 1800–1900*. Cincinnati: Writer's Digest Books, 2001.

Reader's Digest Association. *Through Indian Eyes: The Untold Story of Native American Peoples*. Pleasantville, NY: Reader's Digest Association, 1995.

Shoshone Paiute Tribes of the Duck Valley Indian Reservation. Accessed November 11, 2015. http://shopaitribes.org/spt-15/sptmain.html.

Washoe Tribe of Nevada and California. Accessed November 11, 2015. https://www.washoetribe.us/contents/.

LERNER
e
SOURCE

Expand learning beyond the printed book. Download free, complementary educational resources for this book from our website, www.lerneresource.com.

Further Information

Ducksters: Sacagawea
http://www.ducksters.com/biography/explorers/sacagawea.php
Read all about the famous Shoshone woman who traveled with explorers Lewis and Clark.

Gimpel, Diane Marczely. *A Timeline History of Early American Peoples.* Minneapolis: Lerner Publications, 2015. Learn basic historical facts and important historical dates for five major groups of early Americans, including the nations of the Great Basin.

Goddu, Krystyna Poray. *Native Peoples of the Plateau.* Minneapolis: Lerner Publications, 2017. Explore the histories and cultures of American Indians from the Plateau region of the United States.

"Great Basin Human History"— National Park Service
http://www.nps.gov/grba/learn/education/upload/Unit%206.pdf
Read more about the history of the Great Basin and the people who live there.

I Love History: Utah's American Indian Tribes
http://ilovehistory.utah.gov/people/first_peoples/tribes/index.html
Learn about the five Great Basin tribes that lived in what is now Utah.

Jazynka, Kitson. *Sacagawea.* Washington, DC: National Geographic, 2015. Read about the life of one of the best-known figures of the Great Basin peoples.

Shoshone-Bannock Tribes
http://www.shoshonebannocktribes.com
Read about the history, homelands, and current events of the Shoshone-Bannock tribes on their official website.

Index

Photo Acknowledgments

The images in this book are used with the permission of: © iStockphoto.com/Bastar (paper background); © lienkie/123RF.com (tanned hide background); © iStockphoto.com/JenniferPhotographyImaging, pp. 2–3; © Laura Westlund/Independent Picture Service, pp. 4, 6; © David Stoecklein/CorbisFlirt/Alamy, p. 8; © Robert Shantz/Alamy, p. 10; © iStockphoto.com/stuartbur, p. 11; © iStockphoto.com/BirdofPrey, p. 12; © Buyenlarge/Archive Photos/Getty Images, p. 13; © Marilyn Angel Wynn/Nativestock.com, pp. 14, 16, 17, 18, 22, 24, 27, 29, 38, 39; © iStockphoto.com/Adventure_Photo, p. 19; © Lynn Bystrom/Dreamstime.com, p. 20; Nevada Historical Society, 0. 26; Jim Peaco/National Park Service, p. 28; The Granger Collection, New York, pp. 31, 32, 34; © World Of Raees Photography/Moment/Getty Images, p. 40.

Front cover: © iStockphoto.com/fmbackx.